FINDING OUR TRUE POLITICAL CENTER

FINDING OUR TRUE POLITICAL CENTER

Through the Coming Revolution in Voting

Mike Sawyer

To order additional copies of this book, contact:
Xlibris
844-714-8691
www.Xlibris.com
Orders@Xlibris.com
818277

Contents

ABOUT THE AUTHOR

G ROWING UP MY younger brother, Kevin and I loved the challenge of designing our own games. He went on to run a war game company, but I had higher aspirations. I thought I could apply these skills in theoretical physics. It turned out that the subject matter was just a bit too intense for me, so I would have to settle for more mundane things… things like teaching, insurance and finance. After I retired form Wells Fargo in 2011, I started a blog. One of the subjects I covered was ranked choice voting. I began collaborating with a college professor friend of mine. I soon came to realize that this too was a "game theory" problem, more consequential than board games, more down to earth than theoretical physics, but challenging in its own way.

Game theory is the study of mathematical models of strategic interaction among rational decision-makers. Game theory problems are not easily summed up in neat little packages like $(E = mc^2)$. They involve the uncertainty of human behavior, strategic responses and just too many elusive variables. Now when Kevin designed his game "Napoleon's Wheel", historical accuracy dictated that the odds would favor Napoleon, but it is still a zero-sum game, meaning it will end with winners or losers… no ties, no compromises, no peace negotiations. That's pretty much the way everyone from mathematicians to politicians to voters think about voting algorithms. No one ever considered designing outcomes where everyone comes out with a win. A better model is economics where despite some concessions all parties gain from the trade-offs.

As extreme polarization paralyzes the American political landscape, I would be remiss not to tell the story of how designer algorithms can change that terrain (the field of candidates) so the pieces and players align to form better outcomes for the electorate as a whole... the story of "inclusive voting."

CREDITS

I WANT TO THANK Professor Brian Zurowski, Economics (now in the private sector) for exchanging ideas and playing "devils advocate" thus avoiding more than a few "rabbit holes." Describing the book as a broader lens helping voters see the possibilities for future elections, he encouraged me to go ahead with its publication.

I want to thank Professor Emeritus Kent McClelland, Sociology who I turned to having read some of his well-written articles. He showed me how my first draft was written for myself rather than for my target audience. I was writing to learn rather than learning to write. He told me that by bringing the idea of consensus voting into wider circulation as one way to repair our messed-up political system, you are engaged in a really worth-while endeavor.

Cover design by Keaton Kirby.

REVIEW

*U*NLESS YOU'RE *A math nerd you may find it hard to get excited about algorithms, but Mike Sawyer explains in this book why it's worth paying attention to voting algorithms, especially if you're a voter who's fed up with increasing polarization in American politics. In simple non-technical language, Mike lays out the pluses and minuses of a wide selection of voting algorithms. He shows why our usual system of voting, where the candidate with the most votes can win without getting a majority, can lead to polarization and why ranked choice voting, the system recently adopted in the state of Maine, is an improvement but can still lead to problems. When I read a prepublication copy of his book, the highlight for me was learning about a new algorithm "consensus voting" which seemed to hit the sweet spot of the most pluses and the fewest minuses. If you're someone who cares about politics, this short book is an important read.*

Kent A. McClelland

FOREWORD

IN PHYSICS THE electron is the free spirit, electrically charged, easily energized, appearing to hop randomly from one atom to the next. When discovered in 1897 we really didn't know how we might come to use it. We knew what we were looking for. We had seen its power in lightning storms and captured its energy as it passed through copper wire but no one foresaw the amazing things it would come to do for us once we learned how to channel its energy through the right circuitry. In politics that free spirit is the voter and our long-standing plurality voting method is the old copper wire. But sometimes when we pull the lever, we get "shocked."

Like electrons, voters will seek the path of least resistance and sometimes it seems the whole world's got a stake pulling switches and placing the resistors all trying to herd us in different directions. So maybe it's time to build a new circuit board.

INTRODUCTION

E XTREME POLARIZATION, A problem with no apparent solution has grown progressively worse during our lifetimes. It almost seems to be a flaw of human nature that can only end with the wholesale surrender of one side or the other; in other words never. Putin would say it's an inherent flaw of democracy and he may be right. But I, for one, am not willing to abandon democracy just yet. The founding fathers knew it was imperfect and would always be a work in progress that passed from one generation to the next. Ever facing new challenges it's now our turn to fix it. It may not seem that something as simple as our voting system could be at the root of the problem, but I believe it is.

Can a change in voting methods and procedures help us regain control of how we select our leaders? Can voting algorithms make the process more inclusive of all sides? Can we replace machinations with negotiations on the floors of Congress? Can the way we vote better serve to unite us rather than dividing us? I believe we can do all of these things.

Voters don't really want to elect dividers and extremists. Just ask them. So why do we end up with such polarizing officials? The reason is the plurality voting algorithm doesn't ask the right questions. We're not talking about some complex mathematical formula here. A voting algorithm is generally a few simple words expressing rules easily understood by voters. But the important question isn't "Do we understand the algorithm?" but rather "Does the algorithm understand us?" In other words how well does it interpret the voters' intentions and translate these into a collective will of the electorate as a whole?

We'll look at the pros and cons of the familiar plurality (often referred to as "first past the post") voting method and compare it with instant run-off voting (IRV) which is gaining popularity in several jurisdictions across the country. Often mistakenly called ranked choice voting (RCV), the instant run-off is just one of many voting methods that selects a winner or winners from a ranked choice ballot. Ranked choice voting, as the name implies is any method where the voter ranks his or her choices or candidates in order of preference.

There is a growing consensus among American voters that the current plurality voting system fails us in many ways. We know ranked choice ballots can tell us much more about what each voter really wants. The first goal of this book is to find an algorithm which most accurately interprets each voter's wishes and translates this into a collective decision.

It is important to note that ranked choice voting does not refer to a single method as the public is being told. The public has not really had a chance to compare with other ranked choice methods several of which will better serve the voters. There's an even bigger concern with calling the instant run-off "ranked choice voting." The fact that Democrats and Republicans alike have come to think of instant run-off voting as a scheme to get more Democrats elected, has made this a highly partisan issue. It's clear this was never the intent but the growing perception of partisanship will almost certainly derail the ranked choice movement. For this reason it is urgent we find a fairer algorithm to replace instant run-off voting before it permanently taints the whole class of ranked choice algorithms.

Fortunately there are several better choices to choose from. Remember the instant run-off has become the most popular because it's the first challenger to plurality voting, not because it's the best.

Now I can't compare all the known algorithms, but it's my pleasure to show you a few and highlight those properties which make them good choices or bad choices. Some are well-known to mathematicians, like the instant-run-off, the Coombs method or bad apple sort (BAS), approval voting, STAR voting and negative voting.

While there are several worthy of consideration, I will give my highest rating to a method called Consensus voting. I like it because it demands more than a simple plurality, more than a marginal majority; it demands a consensus among voters.

But let's start by asking what we really want a voting algorithm to do for us.

WHAT SHOULD WE EXPECT FROM A VOTING METHOD?

I'M SURE YOU'RE wondering "How many different ways can there be to count my vote and what difference does it make anyway?" How many do you want? Better yet let's start with this question "What kind of results do you want from a voting method?

Do you prefer one that is more likely to select;

- The candidate(s) nearest the political center of the entire electorate (the centrist)?
- The candidate(s) who best represents the whole majority party?
- The candidate(s) who distinguishes themselves as being farthest from the opposition party (the extremist)?
- And which of these do you think we have now?

Would you like a voting system that attracts more voters to the polls? Would you want it to be simple?

Would you prefer a voting system that gives more weight to the opinion of informed voters?

Do you think a voting algorithm should give more weight to flexible voters?

(i.e. if we gave them a way to say, "I would be satisfied if either candidate B, C or F wins.")

Would you prefer voting system that discourages divisive campaign tactics?

Would you prefer voting system that is more inclusive of all factions?

It may surprise you that accomplishing all of these things and more are possible depending on which sorting algorithms we use to select the winner. It may not come as a surprise that some of these things will be necessary to fend off internal and external threats to democracies around the world.

THE TWO-PARTY SYSTEM

THE TWO-PARTY SYSTEM is the child of plurality voting. Political parties are really just a formal conspiracy whereby similar candidates and their supporters collectively agree to coalesce behind a single candidate to defeat a stronger opponent. Thus was born the primary election. A vote was held among the supporters of similar candidates to see who gets the most votes and all other candidates agree to drop out of the race before the general election.

In theory the two-party system with primaries was to be the solution to the divided loyalties among similar candidates running in the same lane. Losers in the primary must drop out to avoid stepping on each other's toes in a general election.

This so-called "spoiler effect" has often been observed in elections where more than two names were on the ballot. Florida's 2000 Presidential race came down to a 537 margin. As we can see from this chart Ralph Nader competing on the "left" fringe collected almost 100,000 votes while Pat Buchanan on the right got less than 20,000.

PRESIDENT	VICE PRESIDENT	POLITICAL PARTY	POPULAR VOTE	ELECTORAL VOTE
George W. Bush	Richard Cheney	Republican	2,912,790	25
Albert Gore Jr.	Joseph Lieberman	Democratic	2,912,253	0
Ralph Nader	Winona LaDuke	Green	97,488	0
Patrick Buchanan	Ezola Foster	Reform	17,484	0

While common sense tells us if these third party candidates were not in the race, most of Nader's votes would have gone to Gore easily overwhelming his 500 point deficit. But we have to live by the rules we have not the rules we wish we had; at least Democrats do!

Republicans have largely averted the constant threat of candidates rising on the "right" fringe by moving ever more to the right. Otherwise sane politicians try to appease Donald Trump by moving to the right only to find Trump can never be satisfied. Still they see this as the only way to avoid being primaried from the right.

Now the spoiler effect is a problem is unique to plurality voting. Virtually no other voting algorithm exhibits this serious flaw. What we really need to know who would win in various head-to-head matchups and to do this we will need to know something about your second or third choices. Plurality ballots simply don't collect enough information for us to tell. Ranked choice ballots do.

This spoiler effect has been exploited by political strategists in the 2020 election as seen in this story out of Florida

> Frank Artiles, who resigned from his state senate seat in 2017, was charged on 18 March by the Miami-Dade State Attorney's Office for allegedly enlisting a friend with the same last name as a Democratic candidate in a state senate

race in south Florida in an effort to siphon votes from the Democrat to ensure a Republican victory.[1]

Here the perpetrator was arrested, but I suspect he was only caught cheating because the scheme was so blatant. I suspect a more subtle approach might succeed without charges being filed. Does that mean we can look forward to dozens of "spoilers for hire" on future ballots? Would these likely be comprised of pop stars and single issue candidates? If so this dog and pony show would of course be bought and paid for with your donations to the two major parties not to mention all the polling required to determine who can peel away the most votes from your opponent.

The bad news is plurality voting isn't getting better with time. The good news is no matter which ranked choice algorithm we decide to go with potential spoilers become irrelevant.

The spoiler effect is even more profound at the primary level. For instance, in the 2016 GOP primary I was looking for an honest, intelligent, articulate, empathetic candidate with governmental experience and one who had the interest of the American people at heart. Despite appearances that's what a lot of Republicans were looking for. It only makes sense that most of the candidates aspired (with varying degrees of success) to project these same admirable traits. Unfortunately since they were all trying to run in the same lane, they split this vote many ways.

The plurality voting method actually punishes candidates for aspiring to be what most voters want and punishes the majority of voters for all wanting the same thing, in other words for what made them the majority in the first place. Instead a 17% plurality of voters who were looking for a candidate with none of these traits were rewarded because there was only one such candidate. Trump had open lane of his own while competitors were crowded out of the other lanes and out of the race by the spoiler effect.

---

1   The Independent March 20,2021

THE FUTURE OF PARTIES

PARTIES MIGHT NOT have been so detrimental had similar candidates simply organized anew every year around current issues. But perennial parties have become the pervasive forces in politics. Antiquated ideas become entrenched in the party platforms. Policy making is contaminated with money until each party becomes locked in to their own brand of corruption.

My own Republican Party, for instance, has over the years assembled a hodgepodge of policies which no rational mind could ever hope to merge into a coherent philosophy.

And the idea behind parties only works if all party candidates follow the norm (an unspoken rule) of dropping out when they fail to get the most votes in the primary. We saw what happened when Trump merely threatened to run as an independent if he didn't get the full-throated support of the party in 2016.

> *I had to come back and add to this point because of recent events. I know a lot of readers had forgotten Trumps threat to run as an independent in 2016. But now in October 2021, Trump has upped the ante, threatening to have his supporters stand down in 2024 if the party doesn't keep pushing the "big lie." He has also labeled big donors who are holding back, as traitors. I'd like to say "This time he has pushed too far", but I won't risk being wrong again.*

All it takes for a single candidate to bring his own political party to its knees is for him to have a few staunch supporters who would follow his lead splitting the party vote. Can democracy survive when candidates ignore the norms? Perhaps it can, but only if we are willing to abandon the failing plurality system. In the meantime, we may need to learn how to better use its weaknesses in defense of democracy just to counter those who would exploit them to end democracy.

This spoiler effect is a problem only seen with plurality voting. Political parties exist for one purpose and one purpose alone, to counter the spoiler effect by reducing the field to two main candidates. But the Achilles heel of any party is that it relies on honesty and norms to accomplish this.

Almost any other voting method would render political parties pointless. But don't expect parties to disappear any time soon no matter how we might change the election process. Pulling strings and raising money to put new tread on old worn out ideas will keep political parties going for decades to come.

We have seen how one political party has devolved into a collection of cults abandoning entirely norms and principles once held dear just for the sake of winning. While disappointing I can't say it wasn't predictable.

I tried, but found no one with anything good to say about the two-party system.

These ugly trends have more to do with our voting methods than one might think. With a different voting system in place, we might expect to see more independents or third party candidates competing for that "sweet spot" in the middle. Major parties would likely promote multiple candidates in the general election contemplating the possibility that a party moderate might actually fare better with the whole electorate even though party members favored a more right wing or left wing candidate. Later we will discuss "Open primaries", a really exciting proposal that promises to offer us more choices now.

THE GREATEST POLITICAL EVIL

THE FACT THAT so many of the signors of the U.S. Constitution had concerns about the formation of parties, tells me they expected future generations to assess the damage and solve the problems.

> *"There is nothing which I dread so much as a division of the republic into two great parties, each arranged under its leader, and concerting measures in opposition to each other. This, in my humble apprehension, is to be dreaded as the greatest political evil under our Constitution."*

> – John Adams, in a letter to Jonathan Jackson (2 October 1780)

I truly believe we have reached the point where parties will take positions in opposition to the other and hinder its implementation for no other reason than to gloat when it fails. Political points are scored when it fails so they will then do everything in their power to make sure it does fail. Health insurance is a good example of how Republicans in Congress tried to engineer such failure, "failure by design." Of course Adams could never have imagined the vast dimensions of extreme polarization. A swirling polar vortex, it sucks in every imaginable division from black vs white to mask-wearing vs bald-faced.

Theirs was truly an experiment because with no empirical data to guide them, they had no idea when or where something might go wrong. We can't really fault them for choosing the plurality voting method. Without the aid of modern computers and more sophisticated voting methods were simply out of reach.

We now have the tools to analyze empirical data and we've already seen a lot of what can go disastrously wrong. It's our job now to carry on their great experiment forward while preserving the principles of democracy they laid out for us.

Both plurality voting and the instant run-off favor candidates who take these extreme positions in the outer lanes. To counter this we must offer an incentive for moderate candidates to enter the race by opening the center lanes.

The most important part of this job is to find a way to defeat debilitating polarization at the highest levels while accommodating the more commonplace needs of local jurisdictions where experimentation is more likely to begin.

Like a cancer growing at the heart of democracy, it's easy to blame the whole problem on human nature. It's easy to forget there was a time when politics was civil and social norms were understood. But if human nature is the whole problem then Putin is right and we are experiencing the waning years of democracy.

While other considerations must be taken into account, overcoming polarization, uniting the country behind common goals and creating an atmosphere conducive to compromise must be our top priority. So let's begin.

PAIR-WISE VOTING

THE CONDORCET METHOD, often referred to as pair-wise voting can be thought of as the gold standard for voting in certain cases. Say I'm one of several candidates for an office. Polling shows that I would win in a head-to-head matchup against every one of my opponents. If that stands, that would make me what's called a "Condorcet winner." You probably think I should win the election no matter which algorithm is used. Most mathematicians think so too.

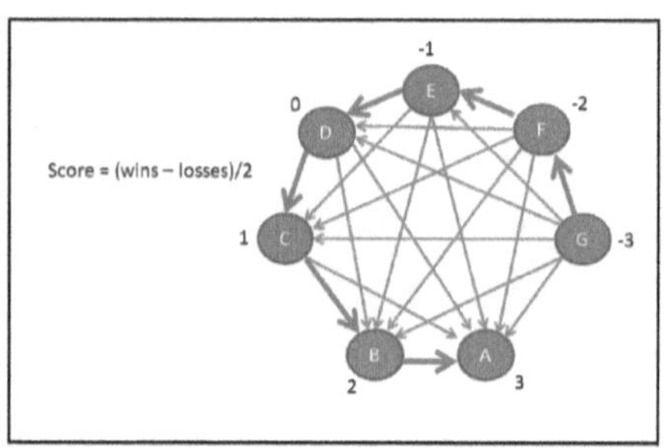

Has a Condorcet winner ever lost a plurality election in the past? It happens more frequently than one might think, especially in polarized races and races where there are two dominant candidates and one or more minor or fringe candidates. The thing is we can never prove that it happened, because plurality ballots didn't collect enough information to tell us if that were the case. But ranked choice ballots do.

The diagram to the left shows a possible ranking on a ballot for a seven candidate race where candidate A is ranked first and candidate G is ranked last. The bold arrows show a single voter who prefers F over G, E over F etc. From these six matchups (bold arrows) we can infer this voter's preference in the other 22 head-to-head matchups (red arrows).

This means we can combine all the ballots to find which candidates win a majority in each of the 28 possible matchups. Ideally we might come up with a collective ranking similar to this diagram where the arrows point to the winner in each matchup. Candidate A beating every opponent is the Condorcet winner while candidate G losing to every opponent is a Condorcet loser. It doesn't always work out this way although it seems like it should. Voting theory tells us that's because voters are "conflicted." I first read to mean a flaw in human thinking, but it may just mean that we rank candidates on a host of issues and prioritize them differently. Let me explain.

Say I am ordering ice cream for a Valentines party. I would choose chocolate over strawberry because chocolate is my favorite flavor. I would choose Strawberry over vanilla because strawberry is red matching the valentine theme. And I would choose vanilla over chocolate because more people enjoy vanilla. I am truly conflicted, but I will find a way to make a decision (we always do) and in fact, I would have to in order to rank these choices.

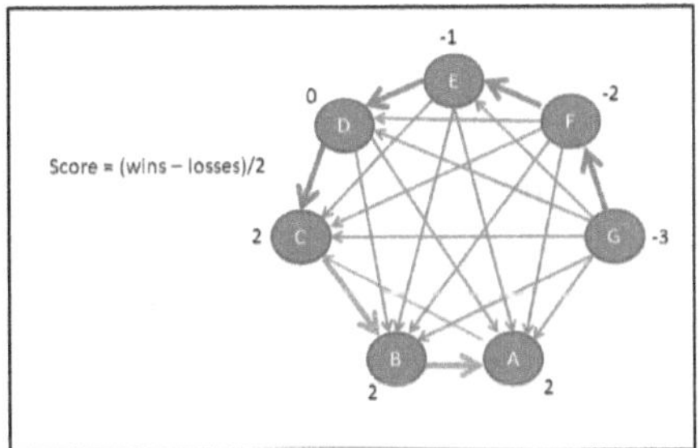

No individual voter can be conflicted because the ballot doesn't allow it. But collectively we can be conflicted. Collectively we can and sometimes do say we like (A better than B), (B better than C) and (C better than A). So whether or not it's due to a flaw in human thinking, we can collectively reach an illogical conclusion. As seen in this diagram, if voters decided they prefer C to A instead of the other way around then candidates A, B and C end up tied for first place. This means pair-wise vote doesn't always find a winner and for this reason it cannot be used as the voting method for an election. It's important to note however that when it does find a winner it provides probably the only completely unbiased standard for selecting an unequivocal winner.

PLURALITY VOTING

__Algorithm;__ every voter casts a single vote and the candidate with the most votes wins.

Profile 1	Profile 2	Profile 3
40%	35%	25%
A	B	C
C	C	B
B	A	A

Head-to-Head Winners

B > A	60%	40%
C > A	60%	40%
C > B	75%	25%

THE SPOILER EFFECT isn't just a fluke. Rather it's a symptom of a method that's fundamentally flawed. We can test this by comparing with pair-wise voting.

In this hypothetical election with three candidates, you rank A first with C as your second choice. 40% of voters fill out their ballots the exact same way. In other words you all share the same voter profile (Profile 1). Judging by the first place votes alone, the voters seem to agree overall preferring A to B and B to C. You have good reason to feel confident that A, the plurality winner is the right choice. But a closer look shows 60% of voters prefer B to A in a head-to-head matchup and 60% prefer C to A. In fact your last pick C is favored over both of his opponents making him the Condorcet winner while the plurality winner, A is actually a Condorcet loser, losing to both of his opponents. Most experts agree that if there is a Condorcet winner, that candidate best represents the wishes of the voters.

And then there's another obvious problem most of us have encountered. Having only one vote, you don't want to waste it. You could end up spending it on the second worst choice only because he has the best chance of defeating your worst choice. Voting often becomes a matter of choosing between the lesser of two evils. Or faced with two bad choices you might even choose not vote at all. Why does this happen so often with plurality voting?

ALL POLITICS ALL THE TIME

T HE U.S. HAS by far the longest campaigning process, among the most adversarial politics and non-stop media and ad coverage; it seems like it's like all politics all the time. Yet we have among the lowest voter turnout in the world. Why is that?

Well for one reason, negative campaigning turns voters off. Turning off the right set of voters is often the key to a successful campaign. To do this it takes lots of time, lots of money and lots of repeating the negative messages. To change this we would have to shorten the length of campaigns, limit campaign contributions and dark money or reduce the effectiveness of negative messages. We've tried and failed on the first two counts.

The secret to achieving the third count is in the "foundational effect" of the ranked choice ballot meaning a candidate may need support from the lower rankings to bolster a win. No candidate comes chasing after my second place vote in a plurality race. If he's not my first choice, he doesn't care if I like him or hate him. Campaigning in plurality race is like building a house with no foundation and selling that house to the public means we bought a house that may collapse with a stiff breeze.

Assuming a candidate does not have an outright majority, he will always need foundational support on a ranked choice ballot to wrap up a win. This is true no matter which ranked choice algorithm we use, but when it comes to counteracting polarization, the choice of algorithm matters.

THE INSTANT RUN-OFF (IRV) OR THE BAD APPLE SORT (BAS)

Instant run-off algorithm; *successively remove the candidate or choice with the* **fewest first place votes** *until only the winner(s) remains.*

(Some jurisdictions use a version of the instant run-off that only allows voters to rank their top three to five candidates)

Bad apple sort algorithm; *successively remove the candidate or choice with the* **most last place votes** *until only the winner(s) remains.*

W E WILL CONTRAST these two elimination style algorithms that look similar but which actually represent two extremes. Unlike pair-wise voting both of these forms express a unique bias. The instant run-off (sometimes called preferential voting or just ranked choice voting) eliminates the least popular choice in each elimination round while the bad apple sort is like repeatedly throwing out the worst apple in the basket until only the prize apple remains.

Whether instant run-off or bad apple sort, elimination rounds are carried out almost instantaneously by computer, but nothing prevents us from seeing what happens round by round.

RCV Ballots Will Attract More Voters

Let's see how this can bring voters to the polls. Compared to other democracies around the world, the U.S. has very low voter turnout. Why? In addition to being turned off by negative ads, too often we just don't believe our votes make a difference. Most voters don't go to primaries where they have real choices and just vote in general elections when the polling is close enough to flip. I think of this as a form of strategic voting.

> ***Strategic Voting*** *– completing one's ballot in a way that does not accurately rank or reflect the voter's true wishes in order to gain some perceived advantage*

Strategic voting always involves some sort of trade-off and destructive forms of strategic voting are always based on a misguided belief that we know how other voters will vote. With a plurality vote I might look past my favorite and vote for someone who's moderately acceptable but who is more likely to win thus avoiding an even worse outcome. In other words I didn't want to waste my vote on what I perceived as a certain loser.

Not voting may also be a form of strategic voting. The perceived advantage here is avoiding "wasting my time" rather than avoiding "wasting my vote" but it's still strategic voting. Political campaigns often take advantage of this natural human tendency by suppressing the vote in key geographic areas. If they can make the task of voting harder and more time consuming more voters will find it prudent and convenient to avoid the polls altogether.

If my favorite candidate has a large lead I may assume he doesn't need my vote to win. The price for this candidate is "free" so I don't need to vote at all. If my candidate is way behind I may think my vote won't help, so I don't vote because he's simply too "expensive." But these do not off-set each other. Let's see why.

There is a good argument that Hilary Clinton lost in 2016 because Democrats stayed home. According to the polls her election looked like a sure thing. So why didn't the Republicans stay home? In this day and age we watch the news media that tells us what we want to hear. That's why CNN could convince Democrats their vote wouldn't even be needed while Fox told its viewers Trump could still win but desperately needed their votes. Both networks were feeding their viewers a heavy dose of optimism. For this reason we should expect the underdog to out-perform polling expectations in a close race. This "underdog boost" may also explain the frequency of very close races.

Ranked choice voting is more appealing to the voter. With seven candidates there must be six elimination rounds. That means that your vote gets used six times and you're likely to win most of them. I consider it a win for any round where your top surviving choice is not eliminated. Of course you must win all six to get your top pick elected, but you only need one win to know your vote made a difference because you eliminated a less desirable candidate. Whether or not your first choice is victorious you still have a say in naming the winner. More voters will vote if they believe their vote makes a difference.

Suppressing the vote means making it harder and more time consuming for the voter. But broader appeal of ranked choice voting will certainly make the task of suppressing the vote harder and more time consuming for Republican controlled state legislatures.

A true democracy invites every citizen to vote. Allowing the state to pick and choose who gets a vote is the first step on the road to authoritarianism.

The Instant Run-off

Maine was the first state to adopt the instant run-off for Congressional seats in the 2016 elections. In one Congressional District there were three contestants, a Republican, a Democrat and a left leaning independent. The Republican had the most first place votes so he would have won in a plurality election. But the instant run-off election meant the independent with the fewest first place votes was eliminated first. His supporters however get to use their vote a second time. So then became the deciders in the election which would be determined by their second place votes. If enough of these votes went to the Democrat, he could overtake the Republican's lead and that's exactly what happened.

In June of 2020 the GOP has succeeded in gathering enough signatures on a petition to prevent ranked choice voting for the Presidential election in November and place the issue itself on the ballot instead. The Republican Party is of course unhappy that their candidate lost but there is some merit in their contention that the instant run-off favors the Democrats, in fact the Democrats think so too. It seems to have this effect because more often than not independents and third parties tend to lean to the left and these voters' second choices decisively favor the Democrats. It's not the argument but rather the perception that this is a partisan issue that will be the downfall of the whole ranked choice movement if we don't act quickly to head this off.

There are many ways to resolve a ranked choice ballot, including some that better reflect the will of the entire electorate in the spirit of weighted compromise rather than a winner-take-all proposition. Two or three ranked choice options should be on the table so we might find one that's acceptable to both parties. The RNC (Republican National Committee) is no more committed to plurality voting than the DNC. They know its flaws as well as anyone.

It's important to note that voting algorithms do not change the behavior of voters, just how their wishes are interpreted. A different algorithm can however change the behavior of candidates from whether they choose to run to how they run their campaigns. They can open the center lanes for many moderate candidates who would not otherwise run for the office. I did say voting methods could discourage divisive campaign tactics. Let's see how the bad apple sort can open an election to a more diverse field of candidates.

The Bad Apple Sort

This is among the most inclusive voting methods. The algorithm successively eliminates the most divisive (most hated) candidates. This process of whittling away at the extreme edges typically finds a centrist or weighted compromise candidate. It also means fewer disillusioned voters will be left out in the cold to become organized dissidents or hate groups. It's especially effective in polarized races.

A polarized race can be easily identified from a set of ranked choice ballots. Typically just two of the candidates share a vast majority of first place rankings, while the same two share most of the last place votes with few in the middle. Apparently voters who like either one of these candidates are inclined (or more likely encouraged) to hate the other. These two candidates typically overshadow the rest of the field. The instant run-off and the bad apple sort operate quite differently in polarized races. Let's see how the bad apple sort opens up center lanes for moderate candidates in such a polarized race.

Imagine an instant run-off election for a certain office is coming up. This is a highly polarized race. We have a conservative candidate "R" on the right pitted against a liberal "D" on the left. D is leading in the polls with the largest number of first place votes.

Candidate D is the projected to win 52% to 48% in this two man race whether the race is determined by plurality or instant run-off. In the meantime a left-leaning centrist "C" is considering running. Candidate C feels that he can attract some of D's first place votes and perhaps a little from R, but only enough to take D out of the lead, not enough to overtake D let alone R. Here is his best case scenario.

With a plurality vote C would be the spoiler for D making R the winner with 46%, but this time we will know for sure a spoiler changed the winner because the ranked choice ballot shows us exactly how this happens.

Profile 1	Profile 2	Profile 3	Profile 4
46%	2%	13%	39%
R	C	C	D
C	R	D	C
D	D	R	R

Head to Head Winners			
D	R	52%	48%
C	D	61%	39%
C	R	54%	46%

Having only 15% of the first place votes, C would be eliminated first in an instant run-off contest, leaving D the winner. It would be just as if C had never entered the race at all. He has no chance of winning either way even though he is a Condorcet winner, favored to win head-to-head matches against both R and D. Now it is common for candidates to run knowing they have no chance (although they will say otherwise). The most common reason is to gain name recognition for a future run. But in this case C has enough name recognition not to want to taint it with a "loser" label. He decides not to run because he has no open lane to run in.

Both plurality voting and the instant run-off are likely to select one of the two most polarizing candidates. They both have a bias favoring extremists. It's just a matter of which one. The instant run-off method seems to be the better of the two. But either way what this means to the voting public is four more years of highly partisan politics.

When C learns this has been changed to a bad apple sort election he sees a possible open lane and reconsiders. We can see that R with 52% of the last place votes will be eliminated in the first round. Once R's last place votes are reassigned, D with 61% of last place votes will be eliminated making C the winner.

Profile 1	Profile 2	Profile 3	Profile 4
46%	2%	13%	39%
C	C	C	D
D	D	D	C

As we look at the first chart, you will see that effectively most of the left-leaning centrists (Profile 3) teamed up with D's supporters (Profile 4) to form a 52% coalition in defeating R. Coalitions between parties are common in Parliamentary style governments. Such coalitions are usually negotiated face to face, but a good algorithm will often do the negotiations for you automatically. In the second chart you will see that even with R gone his supporters are not out; they become the deciders by joining with all the centrists to defeat D.

In a three person race every voter gets to use his vote twice. With the instant run-off algorithm the R voters lost both and the D voters won both creating the perception that it was a scheme to elect Democrats. With the bad apple sort algorithm everyone won either their first or second vote diminishing this perception of partisanship. Even with more candidates two major parties are likely to split the wins and losses fairly evenly. In addition the bad apple sort is more likely to select the Condorcet winner if there is one. If some voter had R and D as his first and second choices he may have lost both, but he can't be all that disappointed with C as a compromise winner.

Not only does C win the bad apple sort race but he appears to do so without running an expensive ad campaign. He is the beneficiary of all the negative ads run by his two polarizing opponents who only succeed in making themselves the two most hated candidates. Now since this is a predictable outcome, this will not really happen. Instead his opponents will have quickly learned not to be so divisive or at least they will have to spread the negativity among all competitors.

A better campaign strategy would be to prove their candidate stands above the rest of the field, not just standing against a single adversary. Not incidentally others who tap into this dissension for personal gain will learn just as quickly. These influencers such as political parties, lobbyists, PACs, special interests, social media, news media and foreign actors have all been known to use hatred and fear to motivate voters often under the guise of "dark money" to hide their identity and true motivations. It makes you wonder how they would spend their money if not for polarization.

Does it make sense that the two most popular (yet most despised) candidates should be eliminated first? It makes sense if you want to elect officials who favor a compromise over a deadlock. It makes sense if you want representatives who will build a reputation on their own merits rather than just disparaging the achievements of their opponents.

Some would argue that in this scenario we could end up electing a doofus who just keeps his mouth shut. Their argument would be borne out by the caliber of third party candidates we've seen in years past. I might however argue that it's no more likely than electing a doofus from a major party and quite possibly one who can't keep his mouth shut.

Even the experts have been too quick to dismiss the bad apple sort based in this "doofus argument." The point is the bad apple sort opens the inner lanes to qualified centrist or moderate candidates who seek to unite us rather than dividing us. While it's true we have rarely seen serious contenders running as independents or third party candidates, we know there are plenty of qualified moderates willing to jump in the race once we can show them an open lane.

The best argument against the bad apple sort may be that it simply works too well.

INCLUSIVENESS

T HE GOAL IS to find our political center and be more inclusive.

Inclusiveness is a measure of how well the voting method weighs the wishes of all factions (including such as racial, ethnic and religious groups as well as party affiliation) in proportion to their numbers to find the right balance.

The bad apple sort is really good at finding that balance, so much so that 435 House members might come to look too much alike. I think of it this way; I could probably eat a supreme pizza for every meal, but I don't. I wouldn't have a healthy balanced diet. We need variety and imagination in Congress to come up with solutions to new problems. On the other hand, if we can't keep our players in the same ballpark we're never going to score. The instant run-off is too divisive while the bad apple sort may be too vanilla; if only we could combine the two.

BALANCED VOTING

F IRST I WANT to mention "negative voting"

Algorithm: *Every voter can either cast his vote for one candidate or against one candidate. The winner is the candidate with the highest point score.*

I won't advocate for this method except to say it's one of the few methods that recognizes these two choices may be of equal importance to voters. But it also suggests that we could do both. Balanced voting is an elimination style of voting on a ranked choice ballot.

Algorithm: *one-half point is awarded for each first place ranking and one-half point is deducted for each last place ranking in every elimination round. The winner is determined by successively removing the candidate or choice with the **lowest point score.***

Thus the average candidate has a score of zero (assuming every voter ranks every candidate). This amounts to a blend of the instant run-off and the bad apple sort. This means a candidate must be concerned with both getting first place votes from his base while at the same time avoiding last place votes from everyone else.

Balanced Voting with its 50/50 split means balanced voting will invite a more diverse field of candidates while rejecting the extremes. Balanced voting does not require voters to rank all candidates. As long as unranked candidates (we call this group the "residual pod") survive elimination, they are all penalized one-half point. This would mean the average candidate would have a negative score.

Balanced voting might be the compromise that most voters can accept, unless we can find a simpler method to accomplish roughly the same thing.

Popularity and Strategic Voting

Many theorists speculate that the bad apple sort method leads to a strategic voting scheme whereby all voters not supporting the most popular candidate place this candidate in last place in hopes of eliminating their most formidable opponent early. That's not quite right. If for instance my candidate is at all similar to the most popular candidate I'm might want to rank this popular candidate second. My reasoning is that voters who dislike him will also dislike my favorite because they are similar. Once he is eliminated my candidate stands to inherent all his last place votes so ranking him second will prolong this hoping to gain more first place votes before this happens. Even if that strategy fails I'm not too disappointed to elect a similar candidate.

It is however a valid criticism of the bad apple sort because some voters will be tempted to deploy this flawed strategy. This strategy may not only endanger their top choice but it unduly punishes popular candidates. On the other hand the instant run-off often overly rewards popular candidates because it counts only first place rankings. But can we find a candidate who is both "generally well liked" like the bad apple sort and who "has a loyal base of core supporters" like the instant run-off? Balanced voting, because it counts both first and last place votes will usually do both.

We know a polarizing candidate who receives half first place votes and half last place vote just ranks near average. So does the candidate with all middle rankings. Chances are that neither of these are good choices. To win a balanced voting contest you will need to score above average through consecutive rounds.

Can We Measure Polarization?

You may think you know a polarized race when you see one and you probably do, but can you really tell whether this election was more polarized than the last? How about the one before that? Is polarization just another one of those immeasurable abstracts like beauty?

I put it more on par with intelligence scoring. We don't really know how to define it, so there's no way to measure it directly. We have to measure instead something that seems to reflect those characteristics we associate with intelligence like the IQ test. The algorithm tends to become the definition. I'm just not aware that anyone has ever tried to do this with polarization

Writing a book about polarization and how to prevent it, without empirical data involves a lot of speculation; let's say a lot of hypothesizing. It involves best guesses about how humans will respond to various stimuli. Humans are challenging subjects. Each hypothesis must be validated by empirical data. What's important to know for now is we can't expect to predict and control run away polarization unless we can measure it in some meaningful way and there is a tool to do just that. Ample data is available in the form of used ranked choice ballots and I've provided a polarization scale as explained in Addendum A of the book.

INDIFFERENCE PODS

ANOTHER WAY OF classifying voting algorithms is whether or not they require "strict ranking", that is no two choices or candidates carry equal value or have the same ranking. Some methods do not require strict ranking or even require similar choices to be grouped together. We call any such grouping of choices that carry equal scoring value "indifference pods" or just "pods" from the old saying "like two peas in a pod." Pods defined by a standardized range of values may be called "pockets." This would include such as an "A" on an exam that might range from 92% to 100% correct. Whether pods or pockets the voting algorithm sees all the choices as identical.

> *Reviving an old joke - A pollster interviewing a potential voter asks "Which do you think is the greater problem with voters, ignorance or apathy?" The voter replies, "I don't know and I don't care."*

But seriously, these are just two possible reasons for voter indifference. There are many more forgivable reasons why voters may have difficulty picking a favorite between two or more candidates in a large field. There are also logical and strategic reasons to separate acceptable choices from bad choices.

The voting methods discussed so far all require strict ranking. The best known exception is "approval voting."

Approval Voting

> **Algorithm:** *Voters can cast one vote for as many candidates or choices as they like. The candidate with the most votes wins.*

There is an approval pod (those you voted for) and a residual pod (all the rest). There are just two ranks, first and last. Obviously this favors the flexible voter who says "I can accept any of these" over polarized voters who are typically obsessed with a single candidate. It also favors informed voters who have taken the time to check out multiple candidates. It may favor intelligent voters who can weigh how to spread their personal influence to multiple candidates, noting you can go too far (voting for every candidate is the same as not voting at all).

Local elections like City Councils or School Boards where there are multiple winners often use some form of approval voting, usually limiting the number of votes you can cast to the number of open seats. Indifference pods allowing two or more candidates to have the same ranks could theoretically be incorporated into instant run-off, bad apple sort or balanced voting if desired by adjusting the algorithm.

Choices always involve trade-offs. The trade-off for the ability to vote for multiple candidates in a single pod is you lose the ability to choose between them. For all its advantages, it's kind of hard for voters to wrap their heads around the challenge of determining how many to approve. So we may need something simpler.

STAR Voting

> **Algorithm:** *Voters rank every candidate by assigning them to one of five pockets giving them one to five points. The candidate with the highest average point count wins.*

Star voting meets one of my key criteria, "familiarity", because everybody has used or read star product reviews like you see in Amazon. It works very well for rating products, because we all share the same general idea of what constitutes a good toaster. The problem is we don't all share the same idea of what makes a good candidate for office. Another reason I don't like it for electoral voting is that voters have a different mind-set when they have to live with their answers rather than just recommending to others.

You place each choice in one of five ranked pockets. Game theory tells me most players (in STAR voting) will choose all ones and fives, making it effectively "approval voting" which is itself a pretty good (and simple) voting algorithm. In a polarized election many voters will rank their favorite as a "five" and give everybody else as a "one" where it begins to look like plurality voting. This "all or nothing" ranking strategy gives their favorite the best chance and unfortunately that strategy is all too obvious. Given a choice between the two I would chose approval voting.

CONSENSUS VOTING

__Consensus Voting Algorithm:__ Voters may rank as many candidates as they wish. Starting with the first tier (all first place votes) we add the votes from successive tiers until at least one candidate collects 60% of the vote or reaches ballot exhaustion. The candidate with the most votes wins.

THE BALLOT ITSELF is no different than the one we are all used to. You simply put an "X" or the numeral "1" in the box next to your top pick just like you would with a plurality vote. But you may also rank your second and consecutive choices on the ballot, as few or as many as you like.

Ballot exhaustion, though unlikely, is when all the ranked choices on all ballots have been counted without any candidate reaching a 60% consensus. For instance, if every voter ranked only their number one choices then it's possible if not likely that no candidate would reach a 60% consensus. The result would be identical to plurality voting except every voter had the option to rank more than one. Even if voter exhaustion should occur it will select the best candidate based of the limited information voters are willing to share.

In fact you can think of consensus voting as a blend between the two most popular forms of voting. If you set the consensus at 0% it would become the familiar plurality voting. If you set the consensus at 100% it would become approval voting. At 0% it's pointless to rank additional choices because the plurality leader has already exceeded the consensus percentage so they won't count. At 100% it's pointless to rank candidates in the approval pod because they all count the same.

Why not set the consensus at the traditional 50%? Well that places us at the greatest risk for a polarized election which, either way, gets us a deeply divided country. If a candidate were to get 51% of first place votes, he is an instant winner. If the other 49% place him last, well we've seen how that divides us right down the middle. You may think there shouldn't be that many really close races, but there are.

That can be partially explained by the "underdog boost", a phenomenon created by political polling and media bias. Today we have the luxury of choosing the polls we like and listening to the news broadcasts we want to hear. If my candidate appears to be winning a race why bother voting since he or she doesn't need my vote. On the flip side if he or she is losing, desperation sets in and I look for a website to tell me what I want to hear, that my vote can make the difference.

If any candidate wins 60% of the first place votes he wins instantly. However when no one gets 60%, we add the second place votes to the total to see if some 60% super-majority (a term borrowed from the so called "filibuster-proof majority" in the Senate) of voters rank any candidates in either first or second place. As many as three candidates can have a super-majority in the second round (3 X 60% is less than 2 X 100%). If more than one candidate reaches this 60% super-majority, the candidate with the most votes wins. If no one reaches 60% we continue adding consecutive tiers until someone does.

Its forthright simplicity, directness and familiarity make it much more likely to gain acceptance by voters and political parties than other more complex forms previously discussed. Just think of it as plurality voting on steroids.

Consensus voting – a universal solution

The more I study voting theory the more I realize how different algorithms do different jobs. The bad apple sort is most effective at finding a meeting time when most members could attend in small groups. It prioritizes urgent preferences such as conflicting appointments over more trivial preferences like sleeping in late, even if a majority prefers to sleep in. Sports broadcasters and gamblers rely on a more sophisticated method called Borda Count because it's been proven reliable in that arena. Scientists will use other complex forms of voting to make collective decisions. But when it comes to electing our officials, voters are skeptical of anything they don't clearly understand, fearing it might be manipulated.

These voters will also resist widespread experimentation with different algorithms. This is why we shouldn't become committed to the first one that comes along. Offer a few options to political subdivisions and voters. Let them sort out what works best for them. Otherwise you can quickly become entrenched in a losing "voting reform" campaign with no way out. To affect change we will need to reach out to both major parties in a bipartisan way to find a method agreeable to both.

It's true we need to act promptly to replace the outdated and misguided plurality voting system, but let's at least take the time to get it right. The transition will go much faster if we give the voters something simple, something familiar and something they can trust in many different voting applications. Addendum B – Predicting bills with bi-partisan consensus discusses how consensus voting might be used in quite different situations.

Consensus voting may be that simple all-purpose workhorse we need.

Consensus voting – intuitive and simple

Consensus voting selects from the top of the ballot rather than eliminating from the bottom. Selecting from the top makes this method more intuitive and understandable to voters. Unlike the instant run-off or the bad apple sort, Consensus voting does not eliminate the "weakest first" or "worst first." All candidates remain in contention until the winner(s) are determined. No matter how far behind a candidate find himself, it's always possible for him to collect enough votes from the next tier to reach a winning majority.

This distinction may seem trivial, but opponents of the popular instant run-off have used eliminations in their arguments against ranked choice voting. For instance <u>Star Tribune</u> Annette Meeks writes in an opinion piece;

> *In ranked-choice voting, sometimes your vote does not count in determining the final winner. That's because you may have selected as your top three choices candidates who are quickly eliminated from consideration. In that case your ballot is discarded and your vote no longer counts.*[2]

Actually Ms. Meeks argument is worse than just trivial, because it demonstrates how ranked choice voting in general is superior to the previous plurality voting system she is defending. With plurality voting if your single choice fails to win a plurality, your ballot immediately becomes useless whereas with three ranked choices your vote continues to work for until all

---

2   Minneapolis Tribune August 10, 2020

three candidates are eliminated. Now the version of instant run-off voting used in Minneapolis allow the voters to rank no more than three candidates. I'm not sure why they limited this to three, but my guess is the wanted to keep the ballot simple.

What is true is that any elimination style algorithm could potentially eliminate a candidate in the first round, who had he survived to the second would go on to win. In fact in a polarized race this is likely to happen.

The consensus voting algorithm never eliminates candidates in the process, so even these arguments cannot be raised. Here's how consensus voting selects a winner without eliminating. Suppose a candidate gets 38% from the first tier and 24% from the second tier. So 62% of voters rank him or her either first or second, a 62% consensus. At the second tier level it's possible that other candidates also have 60% consensuses. In this case the largest majority wins. In a multi-winner race, both or all who exceed the 60% super-majority at the second tier may be winners and we then add the third tier and beyond to find the additional winners.

Consensus voting – more inclusive

We said that polarizing candidates tend to have many first place rankings and many last place rankings with few in the middle. The bad apple sort is inclusive because it eliminates candidates with many last place rankings. While not quite as inclusive as the bad apple sort, consensus voting finds the center in its own way. In a consensus voting contest the polarizing candidate may have the plurality lead in the first tier but be overtaken because he doesn't pick up many additional votes in the middle.

I'm confident that in the 2016 Republican primary Donald Trump would not have had many second place votes. In all fairness he didn't try to pick up second place votes because he didn't need them, efficient if nothing else. I'm just as confident he wouldn't have won the nomination had it been a consensus race. Second place votes are undervalued by the press and the public because they are essentially invisible in a plurality poll. As of late September, 2020 some polling indicated Elizabeth Warren was outperforming Joe Biden when both first and second place were counted even while Biden led with first place votes. That turned out to be short-lived due at least in part to the fact that most polls and elections put all the emphasis on the top slot.

Consensus voting – favors the flexible voter

If you like voting the way you have always voted you'll like consensus *voting.*

If you're a more flexible voter you'll like it even more.

Suppose I was an ardent Trump supporter. For me it was Trump or nothing. I know little about the other candidates and care even less. Well I didn't have to rank anyone but Trump. Why wouldn't I have second choice? Well if I am truly indifferent about the other candidates in the race, then I shouldn't rank them. There is a remote chance that my lower ranked pick will put some candidate over the 60% super-majority first when in fact Trump would have surpassed him on the next tier to go on for the win. This does seem remote, but definitely possible.

Ranking even a few candidates gives more power to flexible voters over voters obsessed with a single candidate. Figuring out how many to rank so as to maximize your voting power (a problem with approval voting) is no longer an issue. Each voter gets the same number of votes counted unless he specifically chooses to rank fewer.

Consensus voting – no need to rank non-viable candidates

Now if you don't want to rank irrelevant or indistinguishable candidates at the bottom of your ballot leaving them unmarked (the residual pod), that's no problem. A super-majority should normally be reached in the first few tiers anyway. Consensus voting avoids entirely the question of how to count last place votes when voters fail to rank all candidates.

Consensus voting – it's scalable

If it seems like 60% is an arbitrary number, that's because it is, but it's the same arbitrary number used in a Senate filibuster where it often blocks legislation. In consensus voting it is used to reach a consensus. There's probably no magic number here but as we have seen 50% is too low and 100% is too high. What we do know is that lower numbers lead to exclusive "winner takes all" elections while higher numbers tend to be more inclusive, more representative of the electorate as a whole.

I can't think of a scenario where we would want to set the consensus below 50% in a single-winner election since it returns us to a situation where the winner could be determined by a simple plurality. Nor do I see much value in setting a threshold above 75%. Note that if every voter were to rank every candidate, then every candidate would eventually reach any threshold since every candidate reaches 100% at the final tier. Since it's unlikely that voters will rank all candidates selecting a higher threshold leaves a greater risk of ballot exhaustion.

Consensus voting and strategic voting schemes

> **Definition:** *Strategic voting means completing one's ballot in a way that does not accurately rank or reflect the voter's true wishes in order to gain some perceived advantage*

The experts would have us think that strategic voting is always a bad thing. Certainly it's a bad thing if it produces unexpected or self-defeating results. It's a bad thing if it's complicated to figure it out. Otherwise it's a choice with a fair and apparent trade-off. Deciding whether to just vote for your top choice or rank additional choices in case your top choice fails is a strategic choice that involves a fair trade off in which different voters may find different choices work best for them. Cooperative schemes such as coercing party members into agreeing to just rank the party's top contender could be considered destructive. Fortunately the secret ballot makes that unenforceable. Besides most voters will vote for additional candidates rather than risk conceding the race to the worst possible candidate if their party's candidate(s) fail to win.

When I started researching voting methods, I assumed that any simple algorithm could be easily played (defeated) by a simple strategy. I was surprised to find that consensus voting seems to be one of the most resistant to destructive or self-defeating strategic voting schemes.

Consensus voting will have critics

But watch their motives and examine their rational. It's not that critics couldn't fabricate situations to provoke doubts like the opinion piece by Ms. Meeks, because they will.

Interestingly in criticizing the instant run-off, she makes a strong case for consensus voting. She claims that some winners of instant run-off races in Minnesota were elected without achieving majority support. Certainly it can be demonstrated that with any voting method that does not require ranking of all candidates it's possible that no candidate gets a majority. However it's impossible for any ranked choice method to perform worse that plurality voting. Since consensus voting never prematurely eliminates a candidate it does the best job of counting every vote to the fullest.

Consensus voting - Summary

In summary here's why I think voters will readily accept CONSENSUS voting.

- It's simple and intuitive
- It's more inclusive
- It's familiar and easy to understand
- It's a workhorse that does many different jobs well
- Voters can rank as many or as few candidates as they please
- Selecting from the top of the rankings inspires voter confidence
- Candidates are not eliminated during the execution of the algorithm
- Every candidate remains viable until a winner is chosen
- It's scalable to make it more or less inclusive
- It's highly resistant to destructive strategic voting schemes
- Voters can think of it as "plurality voting on steroids"

VALUE OF DOWN BALLOT RANKINGS

A MAJOR CONCERN AMONG voting theorist is many algorithms undervalue the second and subsequent rankings on the ballot. Let's see how the algorithms we've discussed preform on this "thought experiment" test.

Imagine a race with several candidates where every voter ranked Jim in second place. Should Jim be the winner? It certainly sounds like he should be. But it depends on what question the algorithm is asking.

Plurality voting asks, "Who has the most first place votes?" so it ignores entirely the merits of a second place ranking.

The instant run-off asks, "Who is liked by the fewest number of voters?" Well, nobody ranked Jim first so he is certain to be eliminated in the first round along with anybody else who had zero first place votes.

The bad apple sort asks, "Who do the voters dislike the most?" We also know that nobody ranked Jim last so he is certain to survive the first elimination round. Nobody ranked Jim second to last either. In fact Jim cannot inherit a single last place vote until the start of the final round. In the meantime Jim (and only Jim) accumulates more first place rankings from eliminated candidates. So the only way Jim could actually lose is if some other candidate, Judy started out with a majority of first place votes from the git-go.

Interestingly, Jim might win even if Judy started out with a majority. It is possible that Judy could be eliminated in the first round having the most (a plurality of) last place votes, even though she has a majority of first place votes. Is this a critical flaw with the bad apple sort? It depends how you look at it. Judy would have to be an extremely divisive candidate to have both a majority of first place votes and a plurality of last place votes. Might it be a better outcome for the electorate as a whole to elect a candidate with broad support through the top half of the ballot than one with enough hard core supporters who muster a majority even if to the detriment of the rest of us? Perhaps we should have asked this question sooner.

Balanced voting asks, "Who has the most favorable balance of likes to dislikes?" While Jim starts out with no likes or dislikes, he inherits likes from every eliminated candidate who has at one first place vote, so he is certain to win if no one started out with a majority. If however Judy starts with a majority, Jim cannot win.

Approval voting asks for "a list of all candidates that meet with your approval." Assuming every voter listed at least two candidates in his approval pod, Jim would receive a vote from every voter so he cannot lose.

STAR voting asks, "Who has the highest average score between one and five?" We can't say for sure, but we can say that if all voters place at least two candidates in the 5-star pocket Jim must win or tie.

Consensus voting asks, "Who has the broadest base of support through the upper tiers?" Barring a candidate who collects over 60% of first place votes, Jim will win with a 100% super-majority in the second tier. Jim may even win over a very divisive candidate who starts with a 51% majority of first place votes.

I imagine that most of you recognized Jim as a likely winner without this level of scrutiny. How well a particular algorithm values down ballot rankings can be the difference between electing a candidate who serves only his base and a candidate who represents all his constituents.

OPEN PRIMARIES

T HIS PROPOSAL IS included as one of the articles of the Anti-Corruption Act (details at anticorruptionact.org) promoted by representUs and others. The Act requires all candidates for the same office to compete in a single, open primary. I would take it a step further and say ranked choice ballots would be the best tool to pare down such a large number of candidates. This could effectively be a dry-run for the general election. Beyond that the possibilities are limited only by our imagination.

Here is the way the people at RepresentUs envision this;

> *A primary election in which all candidates run on the same ballot and the top few vote-getters, regardless of party affiliation, move on to a general election decided with RCV (meaning the instant run-off) allowing for an inclusive primary (for candidates and voters) and a manageable general election ballot.*

When I asked them why their plan didn't call for an RCV ballot to be used in the primary as well they told me;

> *Deciding an open primary with RCV risks overwhelming voters a huge number of (candidates on the) ballots and could increase the risk of ballot exhaustion.*

To be clear this proposed plan was to use plurality voting in the primary and use the instant run-off (RCV) for the general election. My objection is that both of these methods have the same bias, favoring the more extreme elements in both parties leading us once again to a divided government. Ballot exhaustion occurs only when voters do not rank every candidate either because they are only allowed a few choices or because they are unable to rank a large number. With plurality voting you are limited to just one choice while ranked choice often limits you to three or five.

I like the plan but I think we can use ranked choice ballots in the primaries without risk of ballot exhaustion. After all, we shouldn't be expected to know about all the candidates. It's up to the candidates themselves the catch the public's eye. I would substitute consensus voting for instant run-off.

We have already seen how consensus voting will work in an election and reducing it to the five most viable candidates will make it all the better for voters. But what's the best formula for sorting out the best five to move to the general?

Let's say we want the primary to reduce a field of thirty candidates with just five moving on to the general. Obviously this will include several little-known candidates with no real chance of winning and for which voters have no realistic way of ranking. But most of us could pick our top four or five.

Using plurality voting in the primary reveals a problem. In a field of thirty, the top vote-getter would likely have less than 20% of the total vote while the fifth from the top is almost certainly to have less than 10%. This opens the door to hardcore extremist groups. Imagine the American Nazi Party with just 7% percent of the vote getting their candidate into the general election. This is not only unfair to the rest of us, but it wouldn't even be fair to Nazi Party members themselves because their candidate would have no chance in the general election. After all, the point is to move "viable" candidates to the general election.

We might consider a "proportional" system such as the one proposed by FairVote in their pending bill, "The Fair Representation Act." Their formula selects multiple winners based on who has the highest proportion of first place votes. So if we want to select the five winners to move to the general, the first one selected must exceed one-sixth of the vote (if he has more than 1/6 of the vote, there is no way for five others candidates to beat him for the last position). This is also problematic because while maybe the Nazi Party or the Klu Klux Clan can't muster this much support, we know other candidates can attract hardcore supporters in these numbers (requiring at least 17%), such as Bernie followers and Trump followers, neither of whom would be viable in a consensus election. I'm sure many readers will take exception to this but I feel obligated to bring it to your attention.

Consensus voting is the one method most likely to select five viable candidates to move on to the general. Neither Trump nor Saunders is likely to have many second or third place rankings on a ranked choice ballot.

Simply put, performing well in a consensus election means gathering a broad base of support in the first few tiers. The five winners will prove themselves by being the first five to reach a 60% super-majority. Let's look at a hypothetical example with ten choices;

	My ranked choices									
	1st	2nd	3rd	4th	5th	6th	7th	8th	9th	10th
1st tier	22%	7%	4%	21%	6%	16%	1%	2%	2%	19%
2nd tier	24%	5%	3%	32%	9%	18%	2%	1%	3%	3%
Subtotal	46%	12%	7%	53%	15%	34%	3%	3%	5%	22%
3rd tier	9%	16%	3%	14%	15%	18%	4%	3%	4%	14%
Subtotal	55%	28%	10%	67%	30%	52%	7%	6%	9%	36%
4th tier	7%	23%	3%	10%	22%	11%	2%	1%	3%	18%
Subtotal	62%	51%	13%	77%	52%	63%	9%	7%	12%	54%
5th tier	5%	21%	2%	9%	23%	9%	3%	4%	3%	21%
Subtotal	67%	72%	15%	86%	75%	72%	12%	11%	15%	75%

I'm not trying to show any pattern here because I would have no idea of what pattern to expect. Voters are likely to list their preferences honestly because it is too unpredictable to use strategic voting. What I do know is my vote can make a difference and two or three of my picks will likely be winners.

This hypothetical race shows how we might select the top five among the ten candidates. Candidates are identified by the order of my preferences. Twenty-two percent of voters favored my 1st choice putting him or her in the early lead. In a plurality race my first choice would be the winner. But nobody reaches a consensus in the first or second tiers.

After adding the third tier votes my 4th choice reaches consensus to become the first candidate selected (dark shaded). Adding the fourth tier selects my 1st and 6th choices. Adding the fifth tier brings three new qualifiers, but we can only add two, the two with the most votes. My second choice (shaded) qualified by reaching the 60% consensus but was squeezed out because my fifth and tenth choices received more total votes. The fact that my second choice overtook my first choice in the fifth tier is moot because my first choice reached consensus prior to entering the fifth tier. My 1st, 4th and 5th choices made it into the general election and almost got the 2nd. Three out of five is not bad.

Regardless of the number of candidates it's not possible to pick all five in less than four rounds (5 X 60% is not less than 3 X 100%). With consensus voting it is likely that all five winners will be selected by the fourth or possibly the fifth tier, so it won't much matter how you rank the 6th through the 10th candidates or if you choose to rank them at all. I should also note that in this multi-winner version of consensus voting there is still an incentive for political parties to not give their supporters too many choices. In other words, they will want to limit the number of candidates running under the party banner. On the other hand it's more inviting to independents.

Since each successful vote you cast counts the same, it makes no difference in what order you rank your top four picks. As we add tiers, we are essentially building the final approval pod. The number of tiers simply determines how many of my ranked choices get included in the pod, while assuring each voter can have the same number in his approval pod.

Now using the instant run-off might just be the best solution for selecting a winner in the general election. Using consensus voting for both would be like finding the center five then finding the center of the center five. But instead of aiming for the center of the bullseye why not aim for the edge of the bullseye. I like to think the center may where most voters are, but the edge tells where they are going without missing the target altogether. In an ever changing world we need to be prepared to adapt with innovative new policies.

Either way I like the plan. What I don't like is the prospect of getting all the players on board with the plan. Expecting fifty states and one hundred or more state parties to simultaneously adopt this format seems a bridge too far. Maybe we'll get there eventually but I'd like to see it in my lifetime. Perhaps we would be wise to take a lesson Russia to see how disruptive solutions take advantage of the vulnerabilities of plurality voting.

THE SMART-VOTE APP

T HERE ARE SIX parties that hold seats in the Russian Parliament with 48 parties altogether. Putin's party, the United Russia Party is by far the dominant party. Prior to the 2021 election the party was polling at about 30%, but with 48 parties in the mix that should be plenty to keep them in power.

But just to make sure the United Russia Party ran some fake candidates to mess with some Parliamentary election. They also outlawed the strongest opposition party and locked up the some of the strongest competitors including Alexei Navalny who was poisoned and remains imprisoned. To avoid imprisonment themselves, Navalny's organization continues to operate in exile.

Earlier I defined political parties this way.

> *Political parties are really just a formal conspiracy whereby similar candidates and their supporters collectively agree to coalesce behind a single candidate to defeat a stronger opponent.*

This same principle can be reconfigured in many different ways. Navalny's organization came up with something they call "smart voting." They say the only way to hope to defeat the United Russia candidates in Russia's 255 Dumas (think Congressional Districts) is to unite behind the candidate with the best chance to win. To facilitate this Navalny's team analyzed the polling data and published the names of these candidates which could be viewed using the Smart Vote app available in the AppStore and Google Play. This was a very good strategy but only if voters were willing to abandon their chosen party in order to defeat Putin's party. Unfortunately under pressure from the Russian government, Apple and Google withdrew the apps so we will never know how well this might have worked.

What this does show more clearly than ever is that plurality voting strategies are more about defeating a single candidate or party than about electing your favorite candidate. This is true of our primary elections as well. The real goal is not about nominating the most liked candidate in the party but rather about nominating the candidate who can defeat the opposition in the general election.

THE GOOD MISCHIEF CAUCUS

WE'VE SEEN PLENTY of barely legal mischief over the last five years, false claims of voter fraud, severely limiting access to voting, pushing fake candidates with a name similar to an opponent, legislators leaving a state to avoid a quorum, secretly calling a legislature into session without giving enough notice to the minority party and many more. What they all have in common is they are extremely divisive only making polarization worse. Good mischief, however disruptive it might seem, is mischief with the goal of bringing us closer together by helping moderates to win more nominations. It works the same whether we infiltrate the Republican or the Democratic Party. Good mischief is not about Red vs. Blue, it's about extremists vs. moderates.

The strategy is;

Register in the party backing the most extreme candidates and vote for candidates most likely to defeat those extremists in the primaries.

There can't be much doubt even among the Trump base that the most extreme party today is the Republican Party. While good mischief works just as well for Republicans as Democrats, I neither expect nor care if the Trump base were to try to install a moderate to replace an extreme liberal in the Democratic primaries. The Trump base thrives on chaos and prospers with divisiveness so they have no real incentive to adopt this strategy.

Many disaffected Republican voters have left the party and many more are considering it. If keeping your party's registration card meant being loyal to Trump that might make sense, but party registration is just a formality. What it means when sane people leave the party is they are leaving the inmates in charge.

What if there was a way to get disaffected Republicans voters and candidates back in the game? This is essential to achieving your goal, but by itself it won't be enough. So who else would like to embarrass Trump and elect legislators from either party interested in governing? Well, almost everybody!

- Republicans fed up with Trumpism and QAnon because they would like to see a traditional Republican nominee.
- Independents because they want more centrist choices.
- Democrats knowing the Trump base will not show up en masse to support a moderate Republican (or RINO) making him easier to defeat.

We can all benefit from a more moderate Republican Party. Together we might accidentally save the Party.

So why not let our voices be heard where it is most effective? 2022 is the election that will determine the future of Trumpism. Since Trump isn't running his base may not show up in significant numbers. Republicans make up only about 25% of registered voters so acting together as an alliance it is possible for us to outnumber them in their own primary

So how do we coordinate to support the same candidates so we don't split our voting power and how can we know which candidate is most likely to defeat the Trump backed candidate? I would turn to the Republican Accountability Project.

Republican Accountability Project

Their mission statement says in part;
The Republican Accountability Project will:

1. Support Republicans in Congress who, at great personal and political risk, are defying party leadership and defending the institutions of our republic;

Why is this important? Fear of being "primaried" is what keeps Republicans in line with Trump's agenda. If enough of these candidates retain their seats, other Republican may develop the courage to step forward and stand up for the principles of democracy.

> 2. Work to unseat those who have tried to overturn a legitimate election and supported impunity for political violence, including by strategically recruiting and promoting primary challengers through our PAC;

Their mission statement is calling on traditional Republican voters, but that alone is likely to fall short. Remember Republicans make up only 25% of all registered voters, so just a little help from the rest of us can make a big difference.

I wouldn't blame the Republican Accountability Project if they are a little skeptical about non-Republicans volunteering to help their cause. There are some steps we can take to build confidence.

> A. First recruit some of your like-minded friends and select a team leader to minimize multiple requests for the same information.
> B. Collect precinct information for these volunteers so you can make a plan and go to the primary as a group.
> C. Promote our brand #GoodMischief on social media.
> D. Make monthly contributions in the amount of $4.62 (about a dollar a week) as a unique moniker identifying you as a member. If you forget 462 corresponds to the letters GMC (good mischief caucus) on the telephone keypad. This shows them that we are serious about promoting their mission. Bots and pranksters do not make contributions from legitimate bank accounts. That makes it a good way to validate the vote count we can deliver.

With local city and county elections, you're on your own in picking who to support if any. With state-wide elections do some research, check the polling, talk to the local Republican Party office and try to connect with other good mischief groups across the state. Legislative seats and attorneys general positions have become of high importance because these are the people being pressured to overturn elections and negate your vote. Recruit people you know and who believe in democracy to run for these positions. Let the Republican Accountability Project know who you like and why he or she would be the best candidate.

For federal elections the Republican Accountability Project will do the research and you need to follow their endorsements and request connections within your voting district. Every voting district presents a different situation.

Party rules vary from state to state, open primaries can change the calculus in different ways and then there are unique situations such as the Utah race where a moderate conservative, Evan McMullin is running as an independent to challenge the Republican Trump follower Mike Lee.

You just have to decide where your primary vote will do the most good, where it might make a difference and how your vote can bring us together rather than divide us even more.

Republicans should get their house in order first

I've consistently said that voting in the primaries is as important if not more important than the general election, because that's where you have real choices to elect more centrist nominees. So naturally our primaries should be just as secure, but don't take any bets on it.

Let me give you another reason you might want to vote in a Republican primary even when you expect to vote for a different candidate in the general. As participants you can ban together and act together. If you don't like the outcome your participation entitles you to demand an audit. Hell, even if you do like the outcome you can demand an audit just because you think your candidate should have won by more. You will have to make your own "Stop the steal" signs though.

Republicans claim to be concerned, even distraught, over election fraud and they claim to know how to stop it. Then why don't they show us? They can't even get it right here in Iowa where I vote. It's surely important to get it right in the "first in the nation, Iowa caucuses."

The reported count for the 2012 Presidential race in the Iowa GOP primary was that Mitt Romney won the state by 8 votes. Now there is no recount provision for Iowa caucuses, so that might have been it, except for a an oh-so convenient discovery of a 20-point error in Appanoose County[3] that gave Rick Santorum a 12 vote lead. Eight votes was a margin of 0.03%. I figured there were no recounts because of the slip shod way caucuses were run; it would be a big mess. In fact, the vote totals of eight precincts were never counted, so the vote totals are not really known, which makes a fair audit or recount impossible. We don't use voting machines in caucuses. In Appanoose County you would write the name of your candidate on a piece of paper (or two) and throw it in a hat. In other counties it might be done by counting hands, not exactly a secret ballot, but then again you can only cast one vote.

That certainly sounds to me like "just find me 9 more votes in Iowa before the vote count can be certified!" I raised this issue in the 2014 caucuses, but

---

3   **Wikipedia** 2012 Iowa Republican presidential caucuses

I never thought of demanding a recount of 2012. I mean Rick Santorum had no chance at the national convention anyway. In fact, of the 28 delegates sent to the Republican National Convention 22 voted for Ron Paul with complete disregard for the voters of Iowa. He stood no chance either but Iowa GOP voters had to feel their votes were stolen; I certainly did.

"Stop the steal" starts to make a lot more sense when you think of primaries.

PROXY VOTING

W HEN TALKING ABOUT the future of voting we cannot forget about proxies because technology has made it possible to use proxies in ways we never before conceived. A proxy is a legal way to pass your right to vote to another person. It can be restricted to a single vote on a specific issue, commonly used when the person giving the proxy cannot be present to vote. It can also be a blanket proxy passing this right to a series of votes, usually for a set time period.

You might want to think of Congressional District where all Congresspersons carry the proxies for all 744,000 citizens of the district since all districts must be about the same population but this would be the wrong way to think about proxies. A far smaller number actually voted for him or her. The count includes children and aliens who can't vote, a lot who can but simply don't vote and as we have seen the winner may even receive less than half of the votes from those who do vote.

I ran across a voting method called Evaluative Proportional Representation (EPR). The complete algorithm is as complicated as it sounds but included within is a proxy formula, which is as simple as it sounds. The winner who might have received say 250,000 votes is granted 250,000 proxies to use on every bill that comes up in the House for the current term. This would of course mean that states would try to raise voter turnout rather than restricting it. And as a voter who voted for a winner, your vote increases the winner's voting power giving you more incentive to vote even for a sure winner.

If you voted for one of the losing candidates your vote still goes to waste just as it does in any of the single winner-algorithms previously discussed. That is the inescapable tragedy of any single-winner election. With help from social media this notion that "my vote didn't count for anything" had contributed to the rise of dissident groups, intent on taking matters into their own hands as so aptly demonstrated on January 6, 2021.

But even if you voted for a winning candidate you may still lose. He might betray your wishes or just not turn out to be what you expected. After all he or she just has to gain your trust for just one day every two or four years. The rest of the time he spends answering to big donors. If he can't regain your trust before the next election he will resort to running ads depicting his opponent as being "even worse than me." No wonder we call it the swamp.

A proxy in its truest form can be withdrawn making it available to reassign it to another party. No, I'm not recommending yet another way to overturn an election after the fact, but rather a way to reduce a legislator's voting power once in power.

A reassignment of a proxy is quite different than an election itself. It can only be done where there is a legislative body with multiple members of equal rank (a city council for instance). The winner of a Congressional seat would be awarded a proxy for each person that voted regardless of who they voted for. Any voter could then withdraw his proxy and if he chooses reassign to any other member of the House. A voter might choose to be loyal to the local legislator who represents his district or because of his ideology while retaining the option to change his mind at any time. Or a voter can reassign his proxy as often as he wants based on a legislator's stance on bills coming up in the House. So in a way a voter could cast his vote on every piece of legislation that comes before the body if he is so inclined. This could be all done securely using the internet and two-step verification just like a banking transaction.

So I've shown you a way to never let your vote go for naught. Unfortunately it's all a work of fiction; it's never going to happen. But there is a reason I showed this hypothetical process.

DEFERED PROXIES

I N THE REAL world we have to play by the rules we have, not what we wish we had. We don't have a way to take back our vote any time we want. We can't threaten to reduce a legislator's voting power. The best we can do is to say "If you want my support you'll vote yes (or no) on an upcoming bill." I've done that; they don't really care. What they care about is getting the support of big donors to pay for their campaigns.

The Citizens United decision has resulted in the massive amount of corruption and dark money. Big donations can buy a lot of favors. Small donations, no matter how many, cannot be leveraged unless we can find a way to amass them together.

So if I could honestly say "If you will publically support this prescription bill, you will have my vote and a small monthly contribution of $5.00 through election-day and I can deliver 2,500 voters who will do the same. Otherwise we will find a candidate who will." Offering 2,500 committed votes (deferred proxies) plus $12,500 in campaign contributions every month may not seem like much compared to what big pharma can throw into the hat, but that's why we should focus on tight races where the margins are small. Remember too that the money difference doubles between being use for or against the candidate.

Let's understand too that even a small commitment can have a big impact. Unlike anonymous donors and corporate sponsors who negotiate with candidates behind closed doors we have one big advantage they don't. We negotiate in public. We make it known what we have to offer and what we want. Donors want to back a winner, so just the suggestion that they might be competing against even a small organized group of voters and private contribution might make them consider investing their money elsewhere. They have to be concerned because they don't know how quickly our campaign might grow. In fact, the publicity will only help the group grow.

Why not just devote more effort towards traditional activism?

Traditional activism has proven somewhat effective over the years, but you can only take it so far because it is limited in scope. Protests, civil disobedience or letter writing campaigns often fall short, not reaching the people who can really make things happen. Legislators know the people protesting their actions or writing to complain probably won't vote for them either way. We need to confront politicians where they live or die (in the primaries) with what they need to survive (votes).

Many potential volunteers simply don't have the will or resources to join a protest movement. It may require traveling to another location, making protest signs and banners and taking time off from work. It means taking risks. You may be teargassed or arrested by police. You may be assaulted or injured by counter-protesters. You may be harassed online if identified in the crowd by the other side. You may alienate family, co-workers or even your boss. All "good mischief" asks is $5.00 per month and a primary night every two years. Think how many more volunteers might be on board when we show them an easier way to get involved.

Our top priority is to identify the most divisive candidate in every election and take him/her out of the running in his or her own primary or at the very least cripple him. Good Mischief plays out a little differently than the Navalny plan but the cardinal rule is the same "forget party loyalties and support the candidate most likely to defeat the extremist."

SO WHAT CAN I DO?

W HAT CAN I do? I've asked that question myself. As a longtime Republican, I am appalled at what's happened to the party. I fear the gathering storm ahead and a future of civil unrest for my grandchildren. There are many current and former Republicans, who like me have a more clear-eyed vision because we know what the party once was and saw how it went astray. But what can I do?

After all I have but one vote to give for my country. I live in a red county in the red state of Iowa that vote is unlikely to make a difference. This predicament is my inspiration for offering a few ways to make our votes more effective and better reflect the collective will of the people.

What I don't believe in is suppressing the vote with surgical precision to favor one party. I think of those who will not be voting in upcoming elections. If they really don't care, it's probably for the best. I think of my oldest granddaughter who suffers with a bipolar disorder. She won't be voting; she's got her own demons to battle. Believe me, that's for the best too.

I think of those hanging on the brink of sanity, vulnerable to the appeal of mass delusions like QAnon or the daily dose of delusions force-fed to them by FOX News. It seem like the only solution should be some sort of exorcism, a process for driving the evil spirits out of the body of the Republican Party. At the same time, we understand that cloaked in pure insanity there are some legitimate social grievances that must eventually be addressed.

Perhaps we should just treat this as an intervention. You know, the kind of thing you and your friends might do for an old and trusted buddy suffering from an addiction. The hardest part of an intervention is getting up the nerve to gather your friends and discuss how to approach your old friend and that's where "good mischief" comes into play.

It really doesn't matter how you feel about the party because we all have to deal with the Republican Party in one way or another. The question is would you rather deal with a more moderate Republican Party or not?

I have created a Facebook page <u>Finding Our True Political Center</u> for the purpose of discussing the pros and cons of various voting methods as well as ways to make good mischief. Let's use it to challenge each other.

WHERE DO WE GO FROM HERE?

PERHAPS THE BEST forecast of the treacherous road ahead came in an article in my local paper titled *Americans lack trust in government, partisan gap charted*

While 85% of Americans believe it is very important the United States remain a democracy, 52% believe American democracy is facing a "major threat" according to the newest edition of the Grinnell College National Poll (Grinnell-Selzer). The results of the poll, takin Oct. 13-17 (of 2021)… record broad differences between Democrats and Republicans.

The concern that American democracy is facing a major threat is driven by Republicans (71%) and those 65 and older (70%). Only 35% of Democrats say they feel democracy is facing a major threat.

"The sense that democracy is under threat is characterized by deep partisan polarization with Republicans rather than Democrats describing our democracy as facing a 'major' threat," said Danielle Lussier, Grinnell associate professor of political science. "It appears as though baseless accounts of fraud and a stolen 2020 election have

> *sharply eroded confidence in our system among Republicans and created a sense that democracy is facing crisis.*[4]

My biggest concern is that 71% of Republicans think what their party is doing is saving democracy while only 35% of Democrats say they feel democracy is facing a major threat. These are the people most inspired to vote. Are you one of these people?

We can't be frozen by fear of change because one way or another, change is coming. The only question is will you be a part of the force driving change or do you really trust someone else to do it? Together we can forge a new road ahead, a road that brings us back together into a united front, a road that encourages leadership to meet the challenges of the future and a road that creates a government that represents all its citizens.

– END –

---

4   Grinnell Herald-Register October 21, 2021

ADDENDUM A – MEASURING POLARIZATION

WE KNOW THERE is a correlation between "polarizing candidates" and "the winners selected with the instant run-off algorithm." We know there is a correlation between "centrist candidates" and "the winners selected with the bad apple sort algorithm." While we can't measure polarization directly, we can measure the difference in results between these two algorithms on what we might call a "polarization scale." Once we can measure this, we can predict and control outcomes. The hypothesis is that the correlation is close enough that we can predict and control polarization by controlling its corollary.

The measure of polarization on the polarization scale will simply be the difference between the votes received using the instant run-off and votes received using the bad apple sort expressed as a percentage. Vote bias is simply the average between these same two numbers.

ADDENDUM B - PREDICTING BILLS WITH A BIPARTISAN CONSENSUS

A NOTHER WAY TO promote the idea of consensus voting among politicians and legislative bodies might be to offer them a useful tool which will demonstrate the flexibility and effectiveness of consensus voting. This would be a proposal to the House Select Committee on Modernization of Congress.

It is often said of politicians "Pay attention to what they do, not what they say." Perhaps the better question might be "What on Earth are they thinking?" They say what their donors and supporters want to hear and they do what the leaders tell them to do, but at the end of the day they do have minds of their own. So how might we find out what they are thinking and how would that influence what they say or do?

What I am proposing is a simple tool using a consensus voting algorithm to rank a set of pending bills (perhaps 8 to 12 bills) identifying their bipartisan consensus. By "bipartisan consensus" I mean bills on which both parties are likely to agree the bill should pass or they are likely to agree on voting it down thus getting it out of the way, in either a case requiring minimal debate.

Remember this is just a tool to reveal information. What the Speaker, House members or the public does with the information is up to them.

Basically the plan is non-binding with anonymous voting but with a public reading of the total vote count. When a consensus of legislative body comes together (even anonymously) to consider a bill this creates pressure to do it whether or not it's binding. There is a good argument to make it binding to bring a bill to the floor of the Senate where either party can filibuster to prevent any bill from being debated often because their case is weak and debating it would prove embarrassing. The Republican filibuster against the voting rights bill in October of 2021 is just one example.

Each party would choose the bills to be considered in proportion to their numbers in the House. These comprise the set of bills to go on the ballots. All voting members would be required to rank all pending bills in the set. Secret ballots will be counted and sequestered by a non-partisan commission. Only the final results of the vote would be made public.

With a 60% consensus we could guarantee some overlap in even the most polarized House. Say you're a loyal Democrat and I'm a loyal Republican and we each want to support the five bills promoted by our respective parties. For the sake of argument let's say there is no crossover. So after adding our first five tiers we haven't agreed on any of the ten bills. But with the sixth tier all partisan voters must have selected at least two bills in common with every voter from the other party. The bills that end up with the most overlap (receiving votes from both parties) are the most likely to pass with bipartisan support.

In fact we can produce an ordered list starting with the first bill to qualify with a 60% consensus and ending with the last bill to qualify.

A loyal Republican may be inclined to follow the party line, but with a secret ballot he or she may stray a little. Collectively this tendency to stray will foretell movement within the legislative body as well as the party away from or toward certain issues. Even where this representative follows the party line he may prioritize issues in a different order than other Republicans.

Biden's Build Back Better bill is a perfect example where it would be advantageous to have a third party to negotiate with. The negotiation over how much to cut and where to cut, has been a source of great consternation and embarrassment to the Administration. I believe a secret ballot consensus vote on a list of proposed cuts would have speeded up to process by clearly defining what the group as a whole was most willing to cut from the bill.

■